YOU ARE
VALUABLE

.

YOU ARE VALUABLE

DISCOVER WHY YOUR AUTHENTICITY MATTERS

JAKEYA PARKER

Paperback edition December 2021

For information to book JaKeya for your event or about special discounts for bulk purchases, please contact JaKeya Parker by email: info@jakeyaparkerministries.com.

For information about other products and services, visit her website: www.jakeyaparkerministries.com.

ISBN (paperback) 978-0-578-32240-7

Printed in the United States of America

DEDICATION

This book is dedicated to every teenage girl and woman that has struggled with her identity. **You are Valuable.** Always and forever.

CONTENTS

FOREWORD

Everyone has a story. What varies are the events that make up the unique tapestry of the masterpiece of our lives. From developing in our Mother's womb, to our first touch as an infant, to our first step and each incremental step thereafter, contributes to how we see and experience life on our evolving journey. Not everyone is as brave and courageous to share the vulnerable parts of their journey for fear of judgment or rejection. Ironically, we live a more fulfilling life when we are bold enough to speak our truth and free others to do the same. The power of your authenticity can provide a breakthrough for someone traveling down a similar road or prevent someone from taking an unnecessary path. Trauma can be changed into transformation and challenges in choices for growth.

The pages of this book take you on JaKeya's authentic journey of self discovery, introspection and healing. What I know to be true, is you can't fix what you don't face. As you face each part of your journey you become better prepared for your "next" and where it will take you.

To navigate the difficult parts of this journey called life, it is helpful to have a process. JaKeya Parker has developed a brilliant four part system with manageable goals to bolster your process of personal growth and development. In her authenticity lies the language that can heal and support young women of varying ages to grow into better versions of themselves. Those who have had difficult experiences along their journey will realize they are not alone. They will be able to implement the steps JaKeya outlines in each chapter of this book and find strength in knowing and believing the statement **"YOU ARE VALUABLE"**!

Open your heart and prepare to be impacted by the stories and empowered by JaKeya's 4 part system of discovery and why your authenticity matters.

Dr. Stacie NC Grant

Founder, DestinyDesignersUniversity.com

Chief Brilliance Officer, CGEUnlimited.com

PREFACE

BOOM! BOOM! BOOM! I heard a knock at the door. I jumped out of my bed to wake my mother up, but she was one step ahead of me. "Who is it?" Mom asked. As she was waiting for an answer, I peeped around the corner to see what would happen next. "Girl, open this door," the man said. Once I recognized his voice, I became nervous. "You shouldn't be here! Go home before I call the police!" Mom screamed. Within a matter of seconds, my dad forced his way inside and dragged my mom to her bedroom.

Panicking, I started banging on the door as I yelled, "Would you all please stop?! Let her out! Please!" I quickly ran to my room to get my brother, but he didn't care to get involved. He rolled over and went back to sleep as if nothing was happening. I felt helpless! What if my dad kills her? Am I the only one who cares? I thought. As I anxiously stood at the entrance of my room, I listened to my mother fight for her life. I began mentally preparing myself to see a dead body because I could hear her losing oxygen as he choked her.

Suddenly, the doorknob twisted, and the door swung open. By the grace of God, my mom escaped the room and ran out of the house. My dad walked out of the room without uttering a word. He got into his car and left as if he had never been there.

Once my mom saw my dad exit, she came into the house and immediately started crying. As I quietly watched her tears run down her cheeks, my sadness turned into full-blown anger. That was it. My dad was dead to me.

INTRODUCTION

"You alone are enough. You have nothing to prove to anybody."

Maya Angelou

Am I good enough? That's a question that I struggled with for over twenty years. Due to my parents' dysfunctional relationship, I had a hard time understanding love. How could my father say that he loved my mother when he continuously bruised her face? How could my mom say that she loved my dad if she verbally abused him? Was it true love? My curiosity led me to question if my mom and dad understood the meaning of love. If they were struggling to love themselves and each other, how could they love me? And if my parents didn't love me, was I worthy of love?

As children, our parents are the first people to teach us about love. When our parents lack the things we need, they are blind to how their wounded souls damage us. Their brokenness becomes the gateway to our brokenness. Because our parents could not give us what they didn't have, we didn't get what we needed. As a result, countless children have a void that needs to

1

be filled. It is not to say that our parents are bad people, but it's important to shine the light on the truth so that we can deal with the invisible monster, childhood trauma.

Before I continue, I would like to share that I am not a licensed therapist, counselor, or psychiatrist. I am only speaking on this topic from my personal experiences. According to *www.blueknot.org.au*, *The National Institute of Mental Health (USA) defines childhood trauma as "The experience of an event by a child that is emotionally painful or distressful, which results in lasting emotional and physical effects."* Children from toxic backgrounds grow into adolescents and adults searching for ways to hide their pain and fill their void.

My challenges inspired me to search for answers to these seemingly insurmountable problems. After years of research, I have learned that self-worth plays a critical role in what we allow into our lives. Your self-worth determines your decisions, your relationships, as well as the environments you create and partake. Ultimately, self-worth has the power to dictate your destiny. If you are failing to create the life you love, it is not by happenstance. You must become a different person in the process. Bridging the gap between who you are and who you want to be, requires time and work, so I've created a system that will allow you to celebrate small wins along the way.

My system has four parts: self-doubt, self-awareness, self-care, and self-confidence. I'll explain in detail what this may look like so that you can know what to expect. The enemy of your progression is being blind-sighted by the obstacles you could have prepared for in advance. I have learned that it is better to know what to expect when facing challenges than to wish that you knew what to expect. It will save you years of wasted time and energy.

Self-doubt

Doubt is the enemy to your true identity because it is rooted in a lack of trust in yourself. When you can't trust yourself, life will never make sense. It will cause you to live a lie, and the lies will show up in your decisions, relationships, and your environments. They will show up everywhere! Doubt is the invisible force that robs you of the ability to be authentic because you don't know who you are. However, I've discovered that doubt can be an easy fix; owning your truth will force the lies to eliminate themselves.

Part One will teach you to identify and address limiting beliefs, behaviors, or patterns that hinder your growth. In this phase, expect every emotion to start raging because your trauma triggers will surface. Go deeper into the story behind the emotion because clarity cancels doubt. Of course, I am not suggesting that you will never have moments of doubt after this process. I am only suggesting that clarity will uproot the wrong beliefs so that you can create a new belief system.

Self-awareness

You may have noticed that self-awareness began to emerge in Part One, so the work has launched! That's how easy it is to get started. Clarity brings order to confusion, fear, and unanswered questions. It allows you to get to know the *real* you. However, this is *only* possible if you are honest about the good, bad, and ugly parts of your life. As you gain clarity about who you are, your decisions will begin to change for the better. You will make it possible to create relationships that align with your authenticity. You will choose and create environments that support who you are. Ultimately, you will be taking control of your life instead of letting life control you.

Part Two will help you to build the know, like, and trust factor with yourself. If you fail to do this properly, you will allow your doubts to start regaining control over you. In this phase, expect to experience a range of emotions alongside grief. It is normal because there is a tug-a-war that is happening internally and externally. You are bridging the gap between who you were, who you are, and who you are becoming. There are going to be things from your past that must end. Therefore, grief is natural. You will mourn the old you, but you must permit yourself to let go so that you can move forward in your transformation.

Self-care

Transforming into your authentic self comes with challenges that can make you feel depleted because it takes a lot of energy and hard work to heal from your past. I recommend that you make self-care a top priority in your life. Not only is it beneficial in your healing process, but it allows you to show up as your best self in other areas of life, too. Failure to properly execute self-care will cause you to give in to the pressure of your obstacles. As a result, you will slowly move back into the self-doubt phase, believing lies about yourself that are not true. That's the danger of neglecting your needs. You cannot give what you don't have, so become intentional about doing what's best for you. As you practice self-care, you are making sound decisions. You are creating healthy relationships and environments that allow you to thrive. Your intentionality leads to true freedom.

Part Three will teach you how to nurture and protect your mental, emotional, and physical health. In this phase, expect to experience emotions ranging from anger to happiness because you are digging deeper into your past. It will uncover and remove the obstacles that's hindering healthy relationships with yourself and others. Permit yourself to teach others how to treat you by learning how to be good to yourself.

Self-confidence

As you release self-doubt, attain self-awareness, and revive your self-care, you are ultimately restoring your self-confidence. It is where the know, like, and trust factor elevates because you are no longer seeking validation from outside of yourself. You own who you are and that is true freedom. As a result, you are rewarded with sound decisions, healthy relationships, and ideal environments because you did the work!

Part Four will teach you how to enhance your self-worth. Every level will require a better version of you, so you must pursue self-mastery. It will lay a solid foundation for your confidence to evolve. In this phase, expect your emotions to be mainly positive. Believe in yourself, your abilities, and your judgment because you are valuable.

By the end of this book, you will discover why your authenticity matters. You must be ready to do the work to live in your truth. So, this is decision-making time because your destiny is in *your* hands. Allow me to walk you through my journey so you can see what this process did for me. I suggest that you get a pen and your 'You are Valuable' workbook to answer the questions throughout the book. If you don't know the answer to a question, don't hesitate to come back to it later. It will come to you at the right time. You are the answer to your breakthrough. So, let's get started.

PART 1

OWN YOUR TRUTH

OVERCOMING

SELF-DOUBT

A lack of faith or confidence in oneself.
(www.freedictionary.com)

Identify Limiting Beliefs

"You become what you believe. You are where you are today in your life based on everything that you believed."

Oprah Winfrey

I graduated high school, and I encountered a hard decision. I had to choose between college or a job. I was no longer interested in school, so I got a job and an apartment. For some reason, I did not feel satisfied. Why doesn't this feel fulfilling? I wondered. I felt as if my life was missing something. I was doing what I'd seen my mother and grandmother do, but the long work hours changed my views of becoming an adult. The freedom was a plus, but the responsibilities that came along with it were stressful! My intuition told me that there had to be more to life than this, but my environment influenced me to believe otherwise. Therefore, I accepted a lifestyle that I didn't want.

My life was far from the fairytale that I dreamed of because I lived in an apartment that I couldn't afford, worked two minimum wage jobs, and caught multiple Marta buses to get to work each day. At the end of the month, I still didn't have enough

8

funds to pay all my bills. So not only did I have financial struggles, but I also didn't have enough time to enjoy my life. I fell into the horrendous cycle of the rat race, not knowing how to get off the invisible hamster wheel. Thus, I became an angry person.

My anger turned into stress, and stress turned into depression because my life did not make sense. I wanted to be successful like the people that I saw on television. What made them different from my family and I? Did they know something that we didn't? We were just as hardworking as they were, but something was not adding up. I knew something was off, but I had no idea how to solve the problem, nor did I have anyone to teach me. I became hopeless.

We all have the power to create the life we love. However, the challenge is not knowing *how* to do so. Without knowing 'how,' most of us stay in a cycle of sabotage. Our beliefs are so powerful that we will always make decisions based upon them, even if we desperately want better. To change this narrative, we must address our beliefs. The life that you want requires a paradigm shift. Permit yourself to acknowledge and address what's hindering your growth. Here are a few steps that will teach you how to identify limiting beliefs.

Ask questions.

When you are addressing your beliefs, you must know what to ask. Without knowing what to ask, you will not be able to resolve your concern. Question to consider: What do I believe about myself?

Go within.

Once you have identified the belief you want to address, the second step is to go within for answers. You have everything you need to unlock your truth. Question to consider: Why do I believe this about myself? Your diligence will allow you to get to the root cause of the limiting belief.

Evaluate.

Now that you are asking the right questions and seeking the answers to identify your limiting belief, you must evaluate your findings. Questions to consider: What has this belief cost me, and how would my life be different if I didn't have this belief? It will allow you to declutter your mind of all the unnecessary baggage so that you can make room for what you want.

I put my hopes of a better life to the side for the next few years because my hopelessness made me feel like a failure. It became harder to see myself as worthy of anything. I no longer had the urge to try, nor did I want to think about anything, especially problems that I couldn't solve. So, I began to search for ways to cope with my reality. One thing led to another, and I found out the hard way that not dealing with my problems came at a high price.

Identify Low Self-esteem

"We set the standards for how we want to be treated.
Our relationships are reflections of the relationships
we have with ourselves."

Iyanla Vanzant

"In the morning, I'm taking you to see a doctor." Mom said. I didn't utter a word because I knew that I needed to go. We both were concerned about my well-being. My body was aching and sweating profusely. I lost my appetite, and I was fatigued. Once my mom noticed my symptoms, she immediately saw it as a red flag. I had a strong feeling that I knew what sickness I had, but I was afraid to tell her. I thought it'd be best to keep it a secret until further notice.

The next day, we arrived at the doctor's office at 9:30 a.m. As I was waiting for my appointment, my mind was racing with so many thoughts. *What if I have AIDS? Herpes? Gonorrhea?* I thought. Suddenly, the nurse called my name. I followed her to the room and proceeded to tell her about my unusual symptoms. After she finished taking notes, she took my blood work and examined my body parts so my information could enter the lab for testing. They would call within a week for the results.

Within three days, I went to see the doctor. "Ms. Parker, I'm afraid to tell you that you have a bacterial infection, chlamydia, and syphilis," the doctor said. Without flinching a muscle, I uttered one word to him, "Okay." As he continued to address his concerns, the only word that I could hear was "*Syphilis. Syphilis. Syphilis.*" This was worse than I thought, and I couldn't shake the numbness that I felt because I believed that I got what I deserved.

"Keya, what did the doctor say?" Mom asked. "He said that I have chlamydia," I responded. I couldn't fathom the thought of telling her that I was dealing with a deadly STD. I needed time to process everything because I wasn't sure who gave it to me, nor did I know how to tell my former partners to get tested. As a result of my doctor's visit, I received an appointment with the health department. It forced me to break the rest of the news to my mother. She was disappointed in me, but she was more concerned about the necessary treatment to recover, which I did receive.

My self-esteem was tremendously affected by my poor decisions. I thought that I was using sex to relieve stress, but it was much deeper than that. I was covering up the feelings that I didn't know how to express. I felt ashamed and stupid. *How could I allow myself to get to such a low point in life?* I wondered. Deep inside, I knew that I wasn't *this* girl, but my actions always said otherwise.

13

Your limiting beliefs can lead you into the deadly trap of low self-esteem. It is not a coincidence that you are doing things that you aren't proud of; that comes with the territory of unworthiness. Owning your truth will give you the power to change this narrative. Permit yourself to address everything that is negatively affecting your worth. Here are a few steps that will teach you how to identify low self-esteem.

Evaluate your self-talk.

Your thoughts will influence the way that you speak to yourself. Negative self-talk occurs when you are feeling doubtful of your abilities and judgment. You must challenge every belief that is not in alignment with the life that you want to live. Questions to consider: How do I feel about myself? Why do I feel this way? Do I give myself destructive or constructive criticism? What phrases do I constantly repeat to myself? What is my inner dialogue costing me?

Evaluate your decisions.

Once you address your self-talk, you must evaluate your decisions. Questions to consider: Are my decisions helping me to become my authentic self? Why or why not? What are these decisions costing me?

Evaluate your relationships.

Your relationships are a reflection of you. Low self-esteem can influence you to tolerate toxic relationships for weeks, months, and years at a time. You must evaluate every relationship to see how it's affecting you. Questions to consider: Are the people in my life affecting my self-esteem positively or negatively? How so? What are these relationships costing me?

As I committed to deescalate my sex life, I felt a sense of relief. However, it didn't take long for the uneasy feeling to resurface because I didn't solve the *real* problem. I hated to suppress my pain, but it was the only way to keep moving forward. If this was life, I wanted to enjoy it, and I wanted to enjoy it *now*. So, partying with my friends became my new stress reliever.

Identify Negative Patterns

"If you want to fly, you have to give up the things that weigh you down."

Tony Morrison

"JaKeya, I thought you were dead! Don't you ever scare me like that again!" My friend yelled. "I don't mind the tears, but if you can't watch the road, please pull my car over." I responded with a stern tone. I was more concerned about my car than her feelings, and I was wrong about that. She had a right to be upset with me. Minutes before that conversation, two security guards carried me out of the club for passing out because I was too drunk. So, not only did I ruin our night, but I also put myself in danger again.

That would not be the first or last time for my sudden fainting spell, but it wasn't fun anymore. I didn't want to be known for that. I didn't want to be known for drinking at all. It wasn't me. I was so tired of doing things that weren't in alignment with what I wanted. As crazy as that sounds, it was true. I felt powerless.

My friends knew about my struggles, but no one had a solution because we were all struggling with something in a different way. Finding ways to cope with our reality was the easiest way to keep moving forward. That is when I noticed that coping was a lifestyle. None of us were living our "best life", and I could not figure out why. Was this problem more significant than I thought? I had to get answers.

Negative patterns are unnoticed in environments where toxic habits are considered normal. If you are experiencing internal conflict due to your decisions, I encourage you to challenge the norm. We do not need unhealthy mechanisms to cope with reality. We should be able to live a life that we truly want, not a life that we've accepted by default. Here are a few steps that will teach you how to identify negative patterns.

Evaluate your emotions.

When we face seemingly insurmountable problems, we can allow our emotions to get the best of us. The feeling can be so powerful that you would do whatever it takes to suppress or express the feeling. Questions to consider: Are my habits considered unhealthy coping mechanisms? If so, what are they? How do my habits make me feel? Whether your emotions are positive or negative, they have a story behind them. Therefore, you must address the belief.

Evaluate your motives.

Your emotions can and will dictate your actions if you allow them to. Of course, that is not always a bad thing, but it is harmful when your motives are not genuine. Questions to consider: Why do I do the things that I do? What are my triggers?

Evaluate your growth.

Your motives can affect your growth. Therefore, you must evaluate if your patterns are helping you to progress or regress. Questions to consider: Are my patterns helping me to evolve? Why or why not? If I am not progressing, what must I do differently?

That was it. I was finally ready for a real change, and I was excited! Even though I didn't have the answers to our problems just yet, I started to believe that I would find a definite solution. Maybe I could help all of us get on the right path to a better life. With that in mind, I knew the perfect place to go for a fresh start.

PART 2

OWN YOUR THOUGHTS

ACTIVATING SELF-

AWARENESS

Conscious knowledge of one's own character,
feelings, motives, and desires.
(www.lexico.com)

Change Your Mindset

"Step out of the history that is holding you back. Step into the new story you are willing to create."

Oprah Winfrey

*M**y life is not my own. To you, I belong. I give myself; I give myself to you.* As the worship song by William McDowell came to an end, women were crying out to God in prayer. Our guest pastor felt the need to call all of us to the altar for corporate prayer. I got as close as I could to the stage because I was desperate to hear a personal word from God. Standing there with my eyes closed and filled with tears, I silently prayed. Once I finished my prayer, the pastor paced the stage a little bit and passed right by me.

Suddenly, I felt her presence in front of me. She gently laid her hand on my head and said, "Daughter, the Spirit of the Lord comes to you tonight saying, 'it is over. The cycle has broken. The generational curse is coming off of you in the name of Jesus'. I know it hurts, but God says, 'I'm going to use it for my glory. I'm going to be your beauty for your ashes, the oil of joy for your mourning, and the garment of praise for the spirit of heaviness.'

The Spirit of the Lord comes tonight to set you free, and He whom the Son sets free is free indeed. In Jesus' name."

Though I didn't understand the exact meaning of her words, there was one thing that stood out to me. She stated, "The cycle has broken; the generational curse is coming off of you." Those words replayed over and over in my mind for days because I needed to know more. Was *I* called to break the negative patterns in my family? I wasn't sure, but the pastor said it with such confidence that it made me believe her.

After church, I researched curses to get a better understanding of what was happening in my family. There had to be a driving force behind our dysfunction. I no longer accepted it as our fate. I now understood why I felt unsatisfied with our circumstances; it wasn't our destiny. A generational curse is a negative cycle repeated in our families from one generation to the next until someone makes a firm decision to make a positive change. Examples are poverty, addiction, adultery, sexual immorality, lust, anger, murder, arguing, etc. Everything started to make sense, but I had mixed feelings about the revelation. I felt like we were being robbed of our lives in broad daylight, except it was not a gun to our head. It was our decisions that were costing us so much pain.

My desperation quickly turned into inspiration because I wanted to end the bondage not only for myself but for my family and friends, too. It gave me a sense of purpose and hope. Maybe

21

that's what I was missing all along. Perhaps I have been on the hamster wheel all my life because I didn't understand my existence. It was clear to me that somehow, I had the answers for my breakthrough, and it would require me to connect the dots. As a result, our generational curses would turn into generational blessings!

As children, our parents and environments influence our mentality. Once we transition into adulthood, these beliefs impact our decisions. For this reason, everything that you have or lack is shaped by how you perceive yourself and the world. That's how powerful your mind is. Your thought life has gotten you this far, but it will not produce nor sustain the life that you want to create. So, permit yourself to make a paradigm shift. Here are a few steps that will teach you how to change your mindset.

Think.

Now that we've navigated through identifying and addressing your limiting beliefs, it is time to uproot that old belief system! Changing your mindset requires you to install a new belief system that serves your true self. Questions to consider: Who do I want to be? Why is this important to me? How would my life improve with these changes? Make a firm decision about who you want to be.

Act.

As you shift into thinking differently, your actions will need to follow. Questions to consider: What kind of habits do I need to create to sustain my new identity? What can I do to jumpstart my transformation today?

Become.

Would you believe me if I said that you are already becoming the woman of your dreams? By answering these questions, you are proving that to yourself, so I'm proud of you. All it takes is one decision to change the direction of your life. I encourage you to continue going deeper into answering these questions to the best of your ability. As you think differently and act accordingly, you will be one step closer to living the life you love.

Shifting my mindset permitted me to release some of my doubts, and it felt good! It inspired me to go deeper into uncovering my truth, but I felt scared to do so. *Was I ready to talk about the things that I hid for years?* I wondered. Maybe not, but I knew that it was an essential requirement for my transformation, so I opened one of my favorite books and started searching for answers. If I can do the work to change my mindset, I can also do the work to improve my self-esteem. I had a strong feeling that a healthy self-image was vital to break the generational curses.

Love Yourself Healthily

"Dear you,

Stop beating yourself up. No one has ever done this thing called life completely right. Stop comparing your wrongs and focusing on your defeats. You'll never see the strength of your fight until you stop battling your past and start conquering your now."

Sarah Jakes Roberts

"Love is patient. Love is kind. It does not envy, it does not boast, it is not proud. It does not dishonor others, it is not self-seeking, it is not easily angered, it keeps no record of wrongs. Love does not delight with evil but rejoices with the truth. It always protects, always trusts, always hopes, always perseveres. Love never fails." 1 Corinthians 13:4-8 NIV.

This scripture made me speechless because that kind of love didn't seem real. It challenged me to ask myself some uncomfortable questions. Do I love myself? How would I know? I wondered. As I did a little bit of self-reflecting, the uneasy feeling intensified. I had to refrain from suppressing my emotions, so I grabbed my journal to express my thoughts. My letter said these beautiful words:

I forgive you for having a bad attitude throughout the years and not understanding why.
I forgive you for giving your body away to everyone that you've had sex with over the years.
I forgive you for not knowing what you're worth.
I forgive you for not being obedient to God and His word.
I forgive you for not loving yourself.
I forgive you for wasting time that you will never get back because you weren't investing in yourself.
JaKeya, I love you. I always will.

Once I put the pen down, I cried hysterically. I have never felt so ashamed of my life, but this was my truth. I had been running from it for years and I was tired. Who wants to be on the run for the rest of their life? I surely didn't, so I knew that I was doing the right thing no matter how painful it felt. If I wanted to get better at loving myself, I had to permit myself to do so, and so do you.

We cannot give what we don't have. Most of us are pouring into ourselves and others from a state of brokenness. As a result, we damage each other with our wounded souls, and this cycle needs to stop. We should become more intentional about loving ourselves and others from a state of wholeness. However, before we can give and receive love properly, we must first learn to love ourselves. Here are a few steps that will teach you how to love yourself healthily.

Forgive yourself.

Embracing self-love can be challenging, but it is vital for your growth. Forgiveness is required because unforgiveness has been holding you hostage. It blocks your efforts to love yourself healthily. Question to consider: What do I need to forgive myself for at this moment? When you allow yourself to feel the pain you have been carrying around for years, you may have an outburst of tears. Break the silence. Release yourself from the bondage that you are in because you don't deserve that. I don't care how many mistakes you have made. Permit yourself to move on from the past.

Accept yourself.

As you grant yourself forgiveness, it is a must for you to accept yourself. Embrace the good, bad, and ugly things that you discover during your time of self-reflection. Questions to consider: How do I feel right now? Why do I feel this way? What are my feelings communicating to me? No matter what emotions are coming to the surface, allow them to be released so that you can become your safe place. You're not your flaws. You're not your past. You're a woman that was doing the best that she knew how.

Be good to yourself.

Forgiving and accepting yourself will make room for you to be good to yourself. It will move you from a state of brokenness to wholeness. As you are transforming into your true self, please give yourself the grace, mercy, and compassion needed each day; uncovering hard truths is not always easy to do. Question to consider: What must I do to cultivate a better relationship with myself?

Learning how to embrace self-love came with growing pains that I didn't understand. One day, I would feel happy; the next day, I would feel sad. My emotions were so up and down that I thought I was doing something wrong. *Why do I feel like this?*

I'd wonder.

Make Better Decisions

"You are your "why." There is a version of you that you haven't even met yet. That version of you is so powerful. You did not come here to be stagnant."

Sarah Jakes Roberts

My emotions were getting the best of me because I didn't understand why I had mixed feelings. *Shouldn't I be happy with the changes that I'm making?* I wondered. I knew that I was on the right path to discovering my authenticity, but for some reason, I experienced reoccurring sadness, and I couldn't figure out why. I needed assistance processing my emotions, so I called a lady that I met at a gathering.

"Hey darling, how are you?" Natalie asked. I proceeded to tell her about my frustrations to see if she could help me understand my emotions. She responded by saying, "I'm proud of you. It's normal. You are a *Caterfly*. There are others out there that are just like you. Go through your process." I let out a sigh of relief because it finally made sense. I was where I needed to be.

A *caterfly* is someone that is no longer a caterpillar, but they are not quite a butterfly. It's the in-between stage that a lot of us go through. You will know that you're experiencing your caterfly moments when your former decisions, relationships, and environments no longer give you fulfillment. The tug-of-war comes from not knowing where you fit in, and it's perfectly normal. That's a part of becoming your true self. It permits you to build new relationships, create new hangout spots, and find new things to enjoy. So don't fight against your growth by going backward; keep taking the necessary steps to move forward.

I've learned that it's okay to grieve my old life. I am not losing myself; I am simply on the path to discovering my authenticity. Though it is scary and very uncomfortable at times, I've committed to sticking to the process because I deserve a good life, and I have the power to create it. I want to encourage you to be fully present as you transition into a butterfly. Feel every emotion from sadness to happiness. They all play a role in your grieving process. As you permit yourself to embrace the changes, you will move towards acceptance, knowing that you are where you are supposed to be. I challenge you to make decisions that are in alignment with the woman that you want to be. Here are a few steps that will teach you how to make better decisions.

Identify the what.

You must have a vision for your future because your vision will bring clarity to your life and eliminate unnecessary distractions. Question to consider: What do I want? Evaluate that in each area of your life: spiritually, mentally, emotionally, physically, relationally, financially, and economically.

Identify the why.

Your why is the purpose behind everything that you do. So, when you are in the process of making better decisions, you must examine your motives. Questions to consider: Why do I want this? How would my life improve if I had what I wanted? Sometimes we desire things for the approval of others. Your motives will let you know if your desires are in alignment with your true self. If you feel that your why is not authentic, be sure to address the belief.

Execute the how.

Now that you have identified your what and why, you must establish a plan of action. Question to consider: What's the first thing I need to do to create what I want? We often jump into our goals without knowing what to do, where to start, or how to make it happen. Map out a to-do list so that you can strategically achieve your goals. I encourage you to reach out to someone for help in the areas that you need assistance. (My information will be in the back of the book.) You don't have to do everything alone. So take action because the life you want depends on it!

On my journey to making better decisions, I realized that I desired to build better relationships. As I began to do the work, I felt that I was taking two steps forward and five steps backward. Either I was sabotaging my efforts, or I was tolerating people that were affecting my worth. There had to be a limiting belief that I hadn't let go of, and I was right. I still had wounds that needed healing. However, they weren't wounds that I created; it was pain inflicted on me by others. My past had contributed, and I finally dared to go back so that I could progress forward.

PART 3

OWN YOUR TIME

PRACTICING SELF-

CARE

The practice of taking action to preserve or
improve one's health.
(www.lexico.com)

Forgive Someone that Hurt You

"Turn your wounds into wisdom."

Oprah Winfrey

"Girl, you don't listen! You think that you know everything. Get your stupid self out of my face!" Mom yelled. "What? If I'm stupid, you're stupid!" I said without backing down. "Who do you think you're talking to?" Mom asked. Suddenly, we were throwing punches at each other as if we were enemies. I no longer cared about her or her feelings because I was tired of my mom calling me names. So, I decided to protect myself at all costs; it was either her or me, and I chose me.

Fighting with fists and words became normal for us. That is not something that I am proud to admit because it brought me to my knees more times than I could count. I never wanted my relationship with my mother to be that way. However, that was our reality. Even though we love each other, we grew to have a strong dislike for one another. The tension caused our relationship to decline even more. I lost hope.

I began to resent her because she damaged my self-esteem tremendously. As a result, I lost the ability to be kind because I was bitter and angry. My "smart mouth" turned into a defense mechanism to protect my feelings. However, defending myself caused me to disrespect her. This cycle was vicious, and I was over it! I was on the verge of ending our relationship, but it wasn't my heart's desire to do so. Therefore, I knew that I had to forgive her and myself if I wanted to move forward. It was the only way.

Forgiveness can be hard to process because you may feel that the other person doesn't deserve it. However, unforgiveness is blocking your ability to give and receive love healthily. So, not only are you suffering, but your relationships are suffering, too. That's the consequence of unhealed wounds. Some of us may never get the apology we deserve, but we must choose to forgive the other person anyway. I know that may be hard to accept, but it is the gateway to your freedom and peace of mind. Permit yourself to be free from mental and emotional bondage. Here are a few steps that will teach you how to forgive someone that has hurt you.

Process how you feel.

Before you can truly forgive the other person, please give yourself time to process your emotions. Let all your feelings come to the surface, then evaluate how you feel. Questions to consider: What is causing me pain? How do I perceive this pain and why? How would I like to feel? Why is that important to me?

Let it go.

Once you have processed how you feel, you must release all the negative emotions. Remember, you are your safe place. I encourage you to meditate, write in your journal, or use whatever healthy outlet for your peace of mind. Question to consider: What would I have the freedom to do if I were to let go of the offense(s)? Whatever your answer may be, let that be your focus from this day forward.

Move on.

Now that you have committed to letting go of the offense, it is time to move on. This principle will let you know if you have truly forgiven the other person. Of course, this is not an overnight process, but it can happen if you are intentional. Questions to consider: Would I like to continue my relationship with this person? Why or why not? If possible, what can we do to rekindle our relationship? If not, what can I do to keep moving forward?

Forgiveness has taught me to stop living in the past. I am learning how to appreciate my mom and what she has done for me. I must admit that our relationship is still rocky, but there is hope because our love for each other is genuine. Our progress inspired me to analyze my relationship with my dad. I knew this wasn't going to be easy, but it was time.

Heal a Broken Heart

"There are times when we must accept that people are exactly who we hoped they wouldn't be."

Sarah Jakes Roberts

"Keya, get in the car so we can go uptown," my dad said. "No, I'm not going. If my brother isn't going, I'm not going either." I said in a snappy tone. "Girl, get in this car!" My dad yelled back. As I rolled my eyes, I reluctantly made my way to the car so that I wouldn't get in trouble. I hated to be involved with him during his mood swings. Suddenly, his phone rang, and he started yelling at the top of his lungs. There was only one person that could make him act so crazy, my mom. I was used to their chaos, but I didn't understand what it had to do with me. Why did I have to go along for the ride?

Within twenty minutes, we were in the city. As my dad made a complete stop at the red light, he slowly turned his music down and looked over at me. "Get out of the car," my dad said. I looked at him and said, "What? I'm not getting out of this car. Where am I going to go?" The anger in his eyes made it clear that he didn't

37

care, so he opened my door and forced me out of the car. As my bottom hit the ground, he sped off. Tears began to roll down my face because I wasn't sure what to do, but I had to do something quickly.

As the light transitioned from red to green, I was startled by a familiar voice. "Keya, don't you cross that street! I'm coming!" I stopped to look around to find her voice, and she almost wrecked her car to save me. It was my mother, and she was beyond furious! Once I got into the car, she made sure that I was okay. Afterward, she made several phone calls to let out her frustrations. I was so hurt by what he did that everything else about that moment became a blur. My heart grew numb. From that day forward, I continuously asked myself the irresistible question: Am I good enough?

I didn't know how to answer that question, nor did I understand that I had the answer all along. As a result, I unknowingly fell into a vicious cycle of trying to prove to myself and everyone around me that I was worth it. I turned into a people-pleasing, unworthy girl that would do almost anything to keep people from leaving me, especially men. Unfortunately, that toxic mentality became the root cause of a lot of my poor decisions. Though that was a disheartening revelation, I had to release the pain because I no longer wanted my issues with my dad to keep me in bondage. I yearned for true freedom; therefore, I must heal.

Statistics show that millions of kids around the world are the product of fatherless homes. According to *www.fatherhoood.org*, such children are at higher risk for poverty, behavioral problems, substance abuse, child abuse, teen pregnancy, incarceration, criminal activity, etc. We are all affected by the absence or neglect of our fathers, that includes our parents. It's the ripple effect of negative generational patterns. No one gets a pass for mistreating others, but I wanted to give you a different perspective on *our* brokenness. We must heal from our traumatic experiences to allow ourselves to create healthy relationships. As a result, we will end this toxic cycle. Here are a few steps that will teach you how to heal a broken heart.

Forgive

To make healing possible, you must forgive the other person. Questions to consider: What do I need to forgive myself for at this moment? What do I need to forgive this person for at this moment? How does this make me feel? What would I have the freedom to do if I were to let go of the offense(s)?

Tend to your needs.

As you commit to moving on from the offense, I encourage you to practice self-care because dysfunctional relationships can take a toll on your body, soul, and spirit. Self-care will allow you to relieve unwanted stress so that you can focus on building a life filled with love and peace. Questions to consider: How can I improve my mental and emotional well-being? Why is this important to me?

Take it one day at a time.

Healing a deep wound within your heart takes time, so don't rush through your process. Instead, embrace it as much as you can. Love yourself and allow yourself to feel every emotion. Remember, you must be your safe place. When needed, reach out to someone that you trust to support you during this time. You're worth it.

Though I committed to healing from my childhood trauma, I still felt a little uneasy; I was afraid that my parents would do something else that would hurt my feelings. *How could I protect myself if that were to happen?* I wondered. I did not have a solution, so I made a call.

Build Healthy Boundaries

*"You must never be fearful about what you are doing
when it is right."*

Rosa Parks

"Hey, Nat. I have a question. How can I stop my feelings from being affected by my parents' decisions?" I asked in a concerned tone. She responded by saying, "First, I appreciate you for reaching out for advice when you don't know the answer. However, don't keep letting the pain of your childhood drive your emotions. You must know your capacity. Then, work towards setting boundaries so that you can lay the foundation for healthy relationships. Your boundaries will keep the wrong people out, but they will not keep you locked in. Okay? So, let me know if you have any other questions, and keep up the good work."

As our conversation ended, I felt a sense of relief because I finally understood the cause of my frustrations. I tried to create boundaries in the past, but they never seemed to work. One way or another, my parents would ignore my requests. It made me feel like standing up for myself was useless. However, now that I am an adult, this toxic cycle is not beneficial because neglecting my needs is not love. It is death. It was a must for me to teach my parents how to treat me.

My relationship with my dad is mostly non-existent, but we have conversations from time to time. I had to learn that I was causing my suffering because I expected him to be someone that he was not. By knowing my capacity with him, I permitted myself to change how he affected me. Now, when I talk to my dad, I don't expect anything from him. I love and accept him for who he is. That's what matters because I can't change what he did or didn't do. However, I *can* change how I respond.

The relationship with my mother has been complicated for years because of her choice of words. By knowing my capacity with her, I permitted myself to distance myself when necessary to eliminate arguments. I have accepted that some conversations are off-limits if I want to keep my peace. I must admit this has not been an easy transition, but the life I want to live is worth the work, so I have surrendered to my process.

There is so much power in saying NO. It's not rude or selfish to choose yourself when someone is negatively affecting your worth. Sometimes saying no will cause relationships to end, and that is okay. However, if a relationship is worth saving, that is okay, too. You get to decide. That's the power of choice. So, stand up for yourself, even if you are afraid. The consequence of losing a relationship will always be better than losing yourself.

From this day forward, I challenge you to teach people how to treat you. Here are a few steps that will teach you how to build healthy boundaries.

Identify the problem.

Before you can establish a healthy boundary, you need to identify the problem. Questions to consider: What is the cause of my frustration? How does this make me feel?

Present your desire.

Once you clarify the problem, you must identify and present your desire. Questions to consider: What do I want? Why is this important to me? How would the relationship improve with my new boundary? Remember, this is for *your* peace of mind.

Set the boundary.

Now that you have clarified the problem and your desire, you must establish a boundary. Question to consider: What is the consequence of the repeated offense? Be sure that it is something that will hold both of you accountable. However, if they continue to overstep the boundary, that means you aren't keeping your word to yourself. As a result, you will face more internal conflict, and I know you don't want that! I encourage you to make room for people that will love and respect you because you are valuable.

Boundaries are important for every relationship, and that doesn't just apply to people. My unstable relationship with money was in desperate need of healthy boundaries because I reached my capacity with my bills. As a result, I had to face my next challenge head-on.

PART 4

OWN YOUR

TRANSFORMATION

BUILDING SELF-

CONFIDENCE

A feeling of trust in one's abilities, qualities, and
judgment.
(www.lexico.com)

Overcome Life Challenges

*"I've learned that no matter what happens, or how
bad it seems today, life goes on, and it will be better
tomorrow."*

Maya Angelou

"Natalie, I am about to get evicted from my apartment,
and I don't know what to do. I called to see if you
could help me figure this out." I said as I held back my tears. She
said, "Okay. Well, you knew this was coming if you were not
paying your rent. So, start looking for a place before the eviction
is final." Once we finished our conversation, I cried like a baby.
As I wiped my last tear, I took one more look around my
apartment. I finally accepted that it was time to go. I grabbed my
first box and started packing.

I was amazed at how I prospered in one area of life but
suffered in another. It didn't make sense, but I began to realize
that I was the problem. I couldn't blame anyone for the decisions
that I made. My life is my responsibility; I had to accept the hard
truth: I have continuously mismanaged and misused money for
years, which means there is a limiting belief that I am yet to

address.

This eviction taught me that we make life difficult with our ignorance. If I were a good steward of my finances, I would have never encountered this situation at all. That is not to say that I would be free of all problems, but I could have prevented this. My finances have been the number one reason for a lot of my stress. However, money is not the problem; it is my mindset. With Natalie's help, I will face and defeat this giant because poverty is not my portion.

We all have done something that caused us to be in an uncomfortable situation; you are not alone. Reach out to someone that you trust to get the help that you need. I can assure you that this is easier said than done. So please give yourself the grace and time required to work through your situation. Here are a few steps that will teach you how to overcome life challenges.

Control your emotions.

Problems can make you feel overwhelmed and stressed. As a result, you will lose your ability to focus on a solution. Make a conscious effort to stop letting your circumstances control your emotions. You are in control, not your feelings. If you are not happy with your life, it is within your power to change it. See your problems as an opportunity for growth. Questions to consider: How do I feel? What is causing me to feel this way? What must I do to regulate my emotions?

Create a plan.

Once you can think clearly, you must create a solution for your problem. Most of us are unsuccessful at overcoming our challenges because we don't have a vision and a definite plan of action. Questions to consider: What do I want to accomplish within the next 30 days and why? What do I need to make it happen? Will I need assistance to carry out my plan? If so, who will assist me?

Execute.

Now, it is time to act! Questions to consider: What is the most important task(s) to complete first and why? How will I carry out my plan? It may be necessary to do the easiest things first, or you may need to attack the most difficult tasks. Either way, be sure to carry out your plan with a clear strategy. It will allow you to change your situation for the better.

I have always been a person that had to figure out most things on my own, but the trial-and-error method wasted a lot of my time and energy. Because of Natalie, I have learned that I am not alone. I can reach out to her, and she will guide me to make better decisions. We *all* need a support system to help us transition through the ups and downs of life, which is why I value her commitment to me. Our relationship influences me to be better.

Build Healthy Relationships

"You're worth it."

Natalie Fikes

"I don't understand why everything seems to be so hard. When will all of this pain make sense?" I said with a frustrated tone. "It's because you are taking up your cross." Natalie said. As always, we continued to converse about life and purpose until I had the clarity needed to keep moving forward. Once I hung up the phone, I pondered about *my cross*. That statement weighed heavy within my spirit because I knew she referred to Jesus carrying and dying on His cross for us. (For those of us that believe.) Therefore, as a disciple of Jesus, I understood that *my cross* (my pain and suffering) had a purpose behind it. Instead of viewing my challenges as a never-ending problem, I now understand it is a *true* meaning for my existence.

Our conversation brought further clarity to our relationship because purpose is the reason why Natalie and I connected. Her life's journey led her to become a mentor to the youth, giving us the wisdom and guidance needed to can create the life that *we* want. She has become the perfect fit for me as a mentor because I had a lot of trauma to work through. She permitted me to let my little girl cry out because she became my safe place. I no longer had to pretend that I was strong. I could tell her that I didn't know what I was doing, and she didn't judge me for it. Instead, she continued to nurture me with love and guidance. My life has been changed forever because of her service. That's the power of purpose.

Quite frankly, Natalie inspired me to write this book. She knew that other girls and women had stories like my own. I'd connect with them in a way that no one else could. That has become my secret sauce, knowing that my purpose serves a particular group of people. So, not only will I help other women to become their authentic selves, but I will also put myself in a position to end my financial struggles. That's a win-win!

Remember, the people that we decide to live life with are of personal choice. However, it is wise to choose the *right* people to live life with because your relationships have the power to make or break you. Therefore, a relationship with yourself is *most* important. Your relationships will always be a reflection of you. Permit yourself to attract authentic people into your life. Here are a few steps that will teach you how to build healthy relationships.

Seek purposeful relationships.

Building relationships without a definite purpose *for* those relationships will result in wasted time and energy. I encourage you to seek relationships that will help you become your true self in each season of your life. Questions to consider: What kind of people do I want in my life? Why is this important to me?

Understand each other's needs.

Cultivating healthy relationships requires effective communication. Be sure to listen and understand the needs of one another so that you can strengthen the connection. Questions to consider: How can this person be of assistance to me? How can I help them, and why is this important? How would their life improve with my help? Of course, you will need to ask each other these questions, but you need to know *what* to ask when the time is right.

Invest in one another.

You will always know if someone is dedicated, half-heartedly, or not committed to you because their actions will always speak louder than their words, and vice versa. Be sure to be fully supportive of one another so that you can build a healthy relationship.

When I began to understand the importance of healthy relationships, Natalie challenged me to share my life lessons to get comfortable telling my story. I was nervous, but there was no turning back. I knew the perfect place to go to for practice. Ready or not, here I come.

Be Your Authentic Self

"If you are always trying to be normal, you will never know how amazing you can be."

Maya Angelou

"**M**s. Parker, are you ready to present your speech? Remember, you have four to six minutes to tell your story," the host said. I was so nervous that I couldn't speak; I slowly nodded my head in agreement to confirm her words. As she motioned for me to come to the front of the room, my peers gave me a round of applause to show support. It was what I needed to shake off the nervous jitters. Within a matter of seconds, I began to shake uncontrollably, but it was all a part of my plan.

"Would you all please just stop?!" I yelled at the top of my lungs. I paused to gasp for air while my hands continued to tremble. Suddenly, I came to a complete stop and stared into the eyes of my peers. Their silence and undivided attention confirmed that my words had power. At that very moment, I was confident that speaking was something that I was born to do.

After my speech was over, I received feedback on what made my presentation strong, but they also gave me advice for improvements. They stressed that it was pivotal for them to encourage my mistakes while validating my strengths. I couldn't have been happier with the feedback because it reminded me of Natalie. Once again, I felt safe knowing that I could be myself amid my becoming.

So, not only did I fall in love with speaking, but I fell in love with myself more and more. I fell in love with the woman that I am now and with the woman I am becoming. I gave her permission to emerge from the darkness. I gave her permission to leave the past behind. Most importantly, I gave her permission to *live* because I am the light in my own life. I am also to share that light with others. Therefore, I am convinced that my authenticity matters.

Your authentic self is who you truly are, not the woman you have been pretending to be. She is a combination of your past, present, and future self. So, allow yourself to discover who she is. The life that you want depends on *her*. Here are a few steps that will teach you how to be your authentic self.

Know who you are.

Discovering your authenticity will require you to go deeper in your knowledge of yourself. As you go deeper into your awareness, your clarity will intensify. Questions to consider: What do I love about myself? What are my core values? What motivates me? What am I passionate about in life? What are my strengths, weaknesses, likes, dislikes, flaws, and triggers? Be as detailed as possible. Nobody should know you better than you know yourself.

Trust yourself.

As you become sure of who you are through self-awareness, you will permit yourself to trust your decisions and judgment. Remember, you are your safe place. Questions to consider: Am I currently facing any challenges that are causing me not to trust myself? If so, what are they? Am I making decisions that are in alignment with the life that I want? Why or not?

Be yourself.

Being confident and comfortable with who you are, speaks volumes. That is how powerful your truth is. It permits you to be your true self unapologetically. As a result, you will live the life you love. Questions to consider: What must I do to continue living in my truth? Why is this important to me?

Knowing *who* you are and *why* you are is absolute freedom. Not only did my transformation inspire my peers, but it inspired my family, friends, and strangers, too! Who knew that I could make such an impact?

CLOSING

Increase Your Value

"If you are free, you need to free someone else. If you have some power, then your job is to empower someone else."

Tony Morrison

"JaKeya,

In the years that I've known you, I've seen a positive change in you. I would've never guessed that the young and sometimes very angry girl would be this influential, strong, and beautiful woman you are today. You're going to change the lives of so many people. I know it. I can see the drive you have. Continue to grow every single day, and don't ever let anyone hold you back. I can't wait to see where you will be a few years from now. I'm rooting for you!"

Always,

Tee

I never imagined that I would be a woman who others saw as influential. My goal was to change my circumstances by any means necessary because I no longer wanted my childhood to run my adult life. Owning my truth has made this life possible. Who knew that that one decision would lead me towards true freedom? This is the surest I have ever been of myself, but I still have plenty of moments of uncertainty. I know that may sound like a contradiction, but that's what makes me a Caterfly. I am not who I used to be, and I am not entirely who I am becoming. I'm where I need to be. I discovered that my authenticity becomes evident within the journey, not the final destination.

I didn't want to end this book as if I had everything figured out because that's not my truth. I wanted to show up in my most vulnerable state so you would know that I am just like you. We all have things that we must overcome. Some days, I fail in my process, but I never quit because the life I want is worth the work. I'm worth it. You're worth it. My life is not just about me; it's about you and every other woman I will serve.

That's the beauty in knowing who you are; your truth becomes your superpower. I encourage you to stay committed to your process because everybody doesn't need a JaKeya. Some women and men need your story to overcome their challenges. As you create the life you love, I challenge you to teach someone else how to do the same. Here are a few steps that will teach you how to increase your value.

Overcome your life challenges.

Even though a lot of us hate problems, they are of great benefit to us. They teach us how to grow in our capacity, understanding, endurance, amongst many other things. To increase your value, you must consistently overcome the obstacles that you face. Not only will you boost your confidence and success, you will also position yourself as the solution to someone else's problem. As a result, people will come to you for your expertise. Questions to consider: What have I overcome that I would like to teach others? Why is this important?

Refine your gift and skills.

Examine which gift and skill(s) are required to communicate and carry out your solution. Questions to consider: What am I naturally gifted at doing? What skills have I acquired from my past or present job(s)? How can I use them to help others? What draws others to me? Consider every skill that you developed from your current or previous job(s). When necessary, don't hesitate to acquire new skills because they will help you dominate in your sphere of influence.

Serve others.

Now that you know how you're to help others, it is time to serve. As you become your true self, you will learn that life becomes less about you and more about others. Serve others with your gifts and skills because they need you. Questions to consider: Who can I help with what I know? Where will I find them? What kind of product or service are they in need of to succeed? If you need help with any of these steps, please feel free to reach out to me for assistance. I will be more than happy to assist you because serving is what I do best.

I pray that this book has opened your eyes to the woman that God has created you to be. I encourage you to remember that you are valuable not because of what you do but simply because of who you are. Be good to yourself because you deserve it. God bless you. Talk soon.

JaKeya Parker

ACKNOWLEDGMENTS

Without God, I don't know where I'd be. His unfailing love, grace, and patience have carried me many through the ups and downs of life. I'm grateful for my mentor Natalie. This project would not have been possible without her. Natalie, thank you for your wisdom, vision, patience, and commitment to me. I love and honor Ariel, my daughter, who inspired me to become a better woman and mother. Thank you Dr. Stacie for writing my foreword. I'm honored that you said yes! Thank you to my team of experts for the development and production of the book itself.

- My graphic designer, Otis Spears, designed an outstanding book cover.
- My editor, Precious, delivered thorough edits and feedback.
- My interior designers, Jenniii and Accuracy4sure, graced me with their expertise and fast delivery.
- My Photographer, Tim Rogers, shot stunning photos.
- My makeup artist, Morgan, perfected a flawless look.
- My beautician, Alisha, perfected my hairstyle.

Lastly, thanks to everyone who supported me on this journey to discovering my authenticity. Your love and support have been a tremendous blessing! I will always be grateful that I was able to cross paths with each one of you. God bless!

Ja'Urnei	JoTina	Shateea	Cachino
Kevin B	Briana	Allen	Yameka
Kevin C.	Mahogany	Carlton	Jaslyn
Alvin	Stepheny	Loretta	Frank
Teela	Tim	Tanee	Jennifer
Shawn	Alisha	Patricia	Beatrice
Ishaq	Etanya	Morgan	Cathleen
Thadeous	Terrell	Syca	Beatrice
Deana	Christina	Kevin R	Rikkia
Demetrice	Carmella	Ackshun	Paris
Manolie	LaNeise	Marissa	Brandi
Aleia	Ooshie	Kawonna	Mrs. Audra
Dee Bowden	Phil		

About The Author

JaKeya Parker is a Certified Life Coach, Speaker, and Author. She teaches single women how to release self-doubt and discover their authenticity so they can live a life they love on purpose. She is the Founder of JaKeya Parker Ministries LLC. JaKeya is the mother of one daughter and one of four siblings. She is a Christian that enjoys serving God and others. Her mission is to help bring healing and deliverance to women around the world.

To connect with her, visit her website:

www.jakeyaparkerministries.com.

Salvation Prayer

Romans 10:9 ESV says, "because if you confess with your mouth that Jesus is Lord and believe in your heart that God raised Him from the dead, you will be saved."

Heavenly Father, I recognize and know that I am a sinner. I ask that you come into my heart, cleansing me of my sins. Father, I ask you for your forgiveness. Create in me a clean heart. Purify me so that I can live life according to your will. I confess within my heart and my mouth that Jesus Christ is Lord. He died on the cross for my sins and rose on the third day. I accept Jesus as my personal Savior. Father, I believe and receive you, your Son, and your Holy Spirit. I ask that you fill me with your living Word as I commit to a life of following Jesus and serving others. Thank you for saving me. In Jesus' name. Amen.

Prayers for You

Spiritually

Hebrews 11:6 ESV says, "And without faith, it is impossible to please Him, for whoever would draw near to God must believe that he exists and that He rewards those who seek Him."

Father, thank you that your daughter is alive and well. Thank you for keeping her. Thank you for loving her. I ask that you forgive her of all her sins. Father, help her to operate in repentance. May she thirst and hunger after you. Fill her with your living water so that she will never thirst again. Father, your word says that man cannot live by bread alone but by every word that comes from the mouth of God.

Teach your daughter how to build an intimate relationship with you by reading your word and praying without ceasing. Holy Spirit, may you give her divine wisdom, understanding, and revelation knowledge from the word of God. May she learn to walk in Spirit and in truth from this day forward. I bind every evil spirit that is attacking her body, soul, and spirit. I command the spirit of divination, error, torment, strife, anger, fear, and discouragement to depart from her now. I command the spirit of diversion, perversion, poverty, rejection, depression, and abandonment to depart from her now. I command the spirit of doubt, delay, denial, oppression, jealousy, and infirmity to depart from her now.

I command the spirit of death, infertility, bondage, seduction, lust, and unforgiveness to depart from her now. I command the leviathan spirit, python spirit, Delilah spirit, Jezebel spirit, and Ahab spirit to depart from her now. I command marine spirits, familiar spirits, monitoring spirits, and witchcraft to depart from her now. I command these spirits to wither up and die, never to return to her bloodline. Father, I loose your Holy Spirit in her body, soul, spirit, home, ministry, and family. I loose your peace, love, joy, patience, and gentleness in her body, soul, and spirit. I loose your goodness, faithfulness, self-control, kindness, abundance, and good health in her body, soul, and spirit.

Whatever I bind on earth shall be bound in heaven. Whatever I loose on earth shall be loosed in heaven. Therefore, it is so. I prophesy that she will break generational curses. Father, direct her footsteps according to your word and let no iniquity have dominion over her. I stand in the gap demanding justice on behalf of her and her family. Father, your original intent for her was to have dominion in the earth, to be fruitful, to multiply, to replenish, and subdue. Therefore, I evict every evil spirit that is occupying her territories. I command them to get up now. Father put her into her rightful position without delay. Angels, I command you all to defend her and her territories. Protect her body, soul, spirit, home, family, and ministry. Keep her safe from all harm, ruin, and loss. I declare you all successful over the enemy in the spiritual and natural realm. I decree and declare that no weapon formed against her shall prosper. Every plot, plan, twist, scheme, and trick of the enemy will fail!

Father, go ahead of her, be with her, and go behind her. Keep her safe against the fiery darts of the enemy. He is out to steal, kill, and destroy. Open her eyes to his deception, for he is the father of lies. I prophesy that she will hate what is evil and become a lover of truth. Father, make her crooked paths straight. May her will align with yours without delay. You know the plans that you have for her plans to prosper her, not to harm her, but to give her a future and a hope. May the purpose that you have for her be revealed now; your word says that your purposes shall prevail.

I know that you are loving God. You are a just God. You are a God that loves justice and righteousness. As I stand in the gap on her behalf, I ask that you answer my prayers without delay. Your word says the prayers of the righteous person are very powerful in its' effect. Deliver on your promises Father because you are not a man that you should lie. Your word cannot return unto you void. Therefore, you must perform your word because you are faithful. Father, thank you for being El Olam. May she testify of your goodness, in Jesus' name. Amen.

Mentally

> *Romans 12:2 NIV says, "Don't copy the behavior and customs of this world, but let God transform you into a new person by changing the way you think. Then you will learn to know God's will for you, which is good and pleasing and perfect."*

Father, you did not give her a spirit of fear, but of power, love, and a sound mind. Therefore, I curse and bind every thought that is causing frustration, confusion, deception, and doubt. You are not the author of confusion. I loose your word of wisdom, word of knowledge, word of faith, gift of healing, working of miracles, prophecy, discerning of spirits, divers kinds of tongues, and interpretation of tongues in her mind and spirit.

Teach her to bring order to her thoughts now. Bind up every wound in her mind. Uproot every belief that is not in alignment with your will for her life. Guide her through the process of transformation. Strengthen her for the journey. Teach her how to set her mind on things above. Your word says setting your mind on the Spirit is life and peace. I decree and decree that life and peace is her portion now. Restore her mind to full health. Give her discernment to know the difference between your voice and the voice of the enemy.

Teach her to meditate on your word day and night and fix her eyes on your ways. Teach her to be sober-minded and vigilant because the enemy is seeking to devour her. Teach her to put on the full armor of God so that she may stand firm against him. Increase her faith in you because it is impossible to please you without faith. Increase your power within her mind. Make her firm in her convictions for the Kingdom. Teach her to be confident in the woman that you've called her to be. I decree and declare that she is a mighty warrior in your Kingdom.

Give her witty ideas, solutions, dreams, and visions to change the world. I decree and declare that it is so. Father, thank you for being Jehovah Shalom. May she testify of your goodness, in Jesus' name. Amen.

Emotionally

> *Philippians 4:6-7 ESV says, "Do not be anxious about anything, but in everything by prayer and supplications with thanksgiving let your requests be made known to God. And the peace of God, which surpasses all understanding, will guard your hearts and minds in Christ Jesus."*

Father, overwhelm her with your unfailing love. Teach her to love you with all her heart, mind, and soul. I bind every negative emotion, spirit, memory, and circumstance that is causing her not to love. May she cast every care upon you because you care for her. I loose your peace and joy within her soul.

Revive her according to your word. You are close to those who are brokenhearted and save those crushed in spirit. Father, give her a new heart. Remove the heart of stone from her flesh and give her a heart of flesh. Purify and refine her heart daily because the heart is deceitful. Examine her heart to remove everything that is hindering her growth and freedom. Father, deliver her from all emotional bondage. Strengthen her to persevere so that she may be perfect and complete, needing nothing.

Hide your word in her heart. Teach her to be gentle with her words. May she be quick to listen, slow to speak, and slow to anger. Human anger does not produce the righteousness that you desire. I decree and declare that she is emotionally stable. Father, thank you for being Jehovah Rapha. May she testify of your goodness, in Jesus' name. Amen.

Physically

> *1 Corinthians 3:16-17 ESV says, "Do you not know that you are God's temple and that God's Spirit dwells in you? If anyone destroys God's temple, God will destroy him. For God's temple is holy, and you are that temple."*

Father, teach her to respect her body. Reveal to her the proper foods to eat to nurture her body and well-being. I curse and bind every infection, virus, and disease that is in her body. I command them to depart from her, never to return.

Father restore her to full health without delay. Forgive her of every sinful act that she committed against and with her body. Have mercy upon her. Teach her to glorify you with her body. Teach her how to discipline her body through prayer and fasting. I prophesy that she is in full control of her flesh because she lives in the Spirit. I decree and declare that it is so. Father, thank you for being Adonai. May she testify of your goodness, in Jesus' name. Amen.

Relationally

> *1 Corinthians 13:4-7 ESV says, "Love is patient and kind; love does not envy or boast; it is not arrogant or rude. It does not insist on its own way; it is not irritable or resentful; it does not rejoice at wrongdoing but rejoices with the truth. Love bears all things, believes all things, hopes all things, endures all things."*

Father, your word commands that we love our neighbor as ourselves; I ask that you teach her how to do so. I curse and bind the spirit of heaviness, resentment, unforgiveness, and anger against others. I loose the fruit of the spirit within her heart.

Father, forgive her for hurting others. Forgive the people that abused her. Forgive them, for they know not what they do. Open her heart to love wholeheartedly. Teach her to guard her heart. Strengthen her to properly process grief as she lets go of old relationships and memories of the past. I prophesy new relationships with covenant partners. Align her with purpose partners that are in alignment with your will.

Give her discerning of spirits to know the difference between your true children and evil spirits. We are not fighting against flesh and blood, but against principalities, against powers, against the rulers of the darkness of this world, against spiritual wickedness in high places.

Teach her to cast out these spirits because she has the power to do so. Jesus gave us the authority to tread on serpents and scorpions and over all the power of the enemy. Therefore, I decree and declare her victorious over every evil spirit that she will encounter. I prophesy that she will reverse the curses within her bloodline. I command hell to turn her bloodline loose from the kingdom of darkness. May your light shine in the darkness now.

I demand the chains of the enemy to break now. I command her bloodline to arise from the darkness now. I decree and declare that they are coming out of agreement with the devil. I prophesy that his work is finished in their lives. I prophesy that she is taking her rightful place within your Kingdom. Strengthen her for the battles ahead. Perform miracles, signs, and wonders with her life. May her relationships with her family, current or future spouse, friends, coworkers, and covenant partners be united in heart and mind. Father, thank you for being El Shaddai. May she testify of your goodness, in Jesus' name. Amen.

Financially

Matthew 6:33 ESV says, "But seek first the kingdom of God and His righteousness, and all these things will be added unto you."

Father, forgive her for mismanaging her finances. Have mercy upon her. Holy Spirit, teach her how to pray so she can supernaturally change her life. May her actions align her prayers without delay because faith without works is dead. I prophesy that she is wise with her finances. I curse the spirit of poverty in her family. I command poverty to be removed from her bloodline now. I prophesy that she is a lender, not a borrower.

Father, your word says to let no debt go outstanding, but the debt of love. Therefore, I ask that you cancel and pay off every debt that is not of love. Put her in position to be debt-free without delay. Teach her how to manage every resource from this day forward. I prophesy that her bills will be paid off, ahead, and on time. Teach her how to be a cheerful giver because you will bless her abundantly. I curse the spirit of pride, hoarding, and lack. I loose generosity in her mind and heart. Your word says you cannot serve both God and money.

Therefore, I decree and declare that you are Lord of her life and finances. As she surrenders her finances to you, may you give her blessings that are pressed down, shaken together, and running over. Father, thank you for being Jehovah Jireh. May she testify of your goodness, in Jesus' name. Amen.

Economically

> *Genesis 1:28 ESV says, "And God blessed them. And God said to them, "Be fruitful and multiply and fill the earth and subdue it and have dominion over the fish of the sea and the birds of the heavens and over every living thing that moves on the earth."*

Father, reveal your purpose for her life. Create the need for the problems she is to solve. Make room for her gifts in the earth. Give her the vision, clarity, solutions, and strategies needed to dominate her sphere of influence. I ask that you help her create systems for suitability, stability, sustainability, and scalability.

Holy Spirit, teach her how to perfect the vision. I prophesy that she was created for such a time as this. Your word says that creation waits in eager expectation for the children of God to be revealed. Purify, refine, prune and perfect her and the vision you've given her. Reveal her in your divine timing. May she work in alignment with you. Give her peace as she is waiting for your promises. Strengthen her in her weariness. Your word says though the vision tarry, wait for it because it will surely come to pass. I decree and declare that her business will prosper because you will establish the work of her hands.

Father, make her successful in everything she does for your Kingdom. Do the impossible within her life and business so that you are glorified. I prophesy that she will make sound decisions for her business. I prophesy that she will operate with integrity. I prophesy that she will be an influencer, bringing more souls into your Kingdom. Send her the right people in each season to help her succeed. Send her to the right environments for her purpose, callings, and assignments.

Keep her safe from all harm, ruin, and loss. I decree and declare that no weapon formed against her or her business shall prosper. I decree and declare that she will prosper in each season despite the economic state of the world. Provide her with every resource needed to fulfill her destiny. Father, thank you for being Jehovah Shammah. May she testify of your goodness, in Jesus' name. Amen.

God bless you.

Did you enjoy this book?

Here are three different ways that you can help to promote it. Choose what is best for you.

1. Take a picture of yourself and the book. Post it to your social media. Please be sure to tag JaKeya on Facebook and Instagram @iamjakeya. Add hashtag #youarevaluable.

2. Write a review on Amazon.

3. Gift the book to someone that will benefit from the principles.

Thank you for partnering with us!

Made in the USA
Middletown, DE
18 February 2022